TO:

_____

FROM:

_____

Jesus said, "Let the little children come to me, and do not hinder them, for the Kingdom of Heaven belongs to such as these."

This book is dedicated to all the little children around the world whom Jesus loves so dearly and those who teach them to pray.

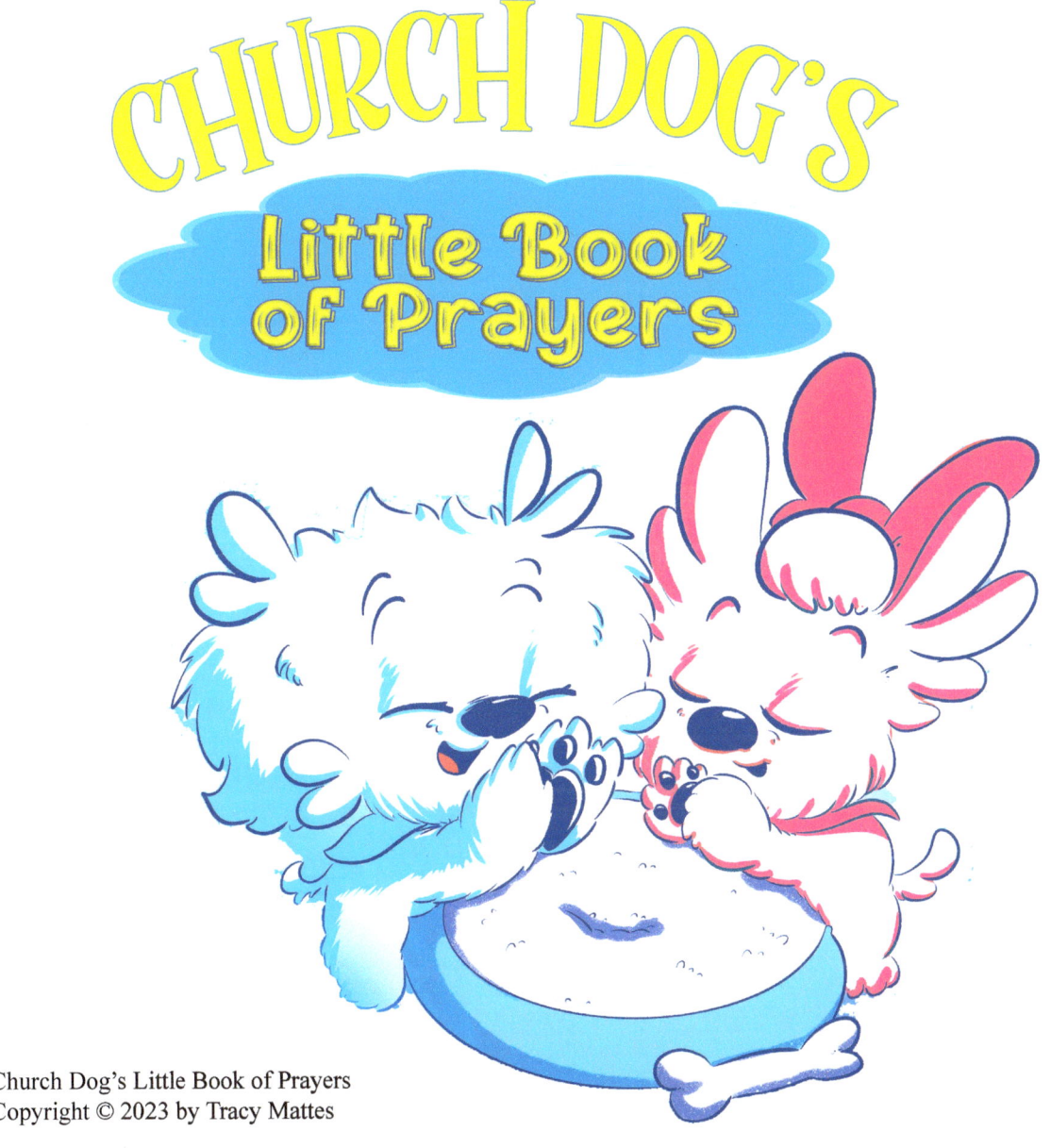

Church Dog's Little Book of Prayers
Copyright © 2023 by Tracy Mattes

All rights reserved. No part of this book may be reproduced, stored in retrieval systems, or transmitted in any form by any means, electronic, mechanical, photocopying, recording, or otherwise, without prior permission of the author, except as provided by USA copyright law.

First Printing 2023

ISBN: 979-8-9873813-3-5

Jesus Keep Me Close

Jesus keep me close to You,
and I won't be afraid.
I trust in You to guide me,
as I start my day.
Give me strength to be my best,
I'll try with all my might.
Just knowing You are at my side
makes everything alright.

"Draw close to God,
and He will draw close to You."
James 4:8

Bedtime Prayer

God, when I'm tucked up in my bed,
I feel so safe and sound.
I know that I'm protected
whenever You're around.
You watch me close from up above
and cover me with Your sweet love.
Your angels guard me through the night
and keep me safe 'til morning's light.

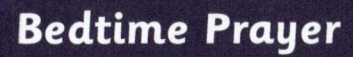

God's Word

God, when I have questions
or I'm unsure of what to do,
I know I can believe Your words;
every single one is true.
Your words shine like the brightest sun
and help me find my way.
Thank You for Your guiding light,
each and every day.

"Thy word is a lamp unto my feet,
and a light unto my path."
Psalm 119:105

Jesus' Little Lamb

Jesus, I am Your little lamb,
I'll follow where You lead.
You always keep me in Your care,
You give me all I need.
If I wander off the path
or find myself alone,
my Shepherd will come to find me
and carry me back home.

Wrapped in God's Love

Your love is like my blankie,
it makes me feel safe.
Warm and fuzzy thoughts of You
help increase my faith.
Protected by Your loving arms,
You're with me day and night.
And when I'm wrapped in Your tender love,
everything feels right.

"God, Your love is so precious!
You protect people as a bird protects her young under her wings."
Psalm 36:7

"Honor your father and your mother."
Exodus 20:12

Blessing for Mom & Dad

God, thank You for my mom and dad,
they are my biggest fans.
They cheer me on to do my best,
they show me that I can.
They love me and work hard each day,
to take care of all my needs.
Please bless them, Lord, one hundred-fold,
for how much they've blessed me.

My Best Friend Jesus

Jesus, I've never had a friend
as wonderful as You.
You're there for me and love me,
no matter what I do.
Will You please remind me
when I feel sad or all alone,
to talk to You, my special friend,
the best I've ever known.

"Jesus stood up and commanded the wind and the waves to stop. He said, 'Quiet! Be still!' Then the wind stopped, and the lake became calm."

Mark 4:39

Prayer During a Storm

Jesus hold my hand, please don't let me go.
The thunder's getting closer, as rain and cold winds blow.
Protect my family, friends and home,
thank You that I am not alone.
With You, I feel safe and warm.
I know that You can calm the storm.
As long as You're here, I won't be afraid,
because the wind and waves still know Your name.

Prayer for Forgiveness

Jesus, please forgive me,
I made mistakes today.
It wasn't my intention,
it just turned out that way.
I know that I can come to You
and tell You what went wrong.
You'll show me how to change my ways
so next time I'll be strong.

"The life of every creature and the breath
of all people are in God's hand."
Job 12:10

Prayer for Pets

Thank You, God, for our sweet pets,
for kittens and for dogs,
For little hamsters, pretty ponies,
and happy leaping frogs.
Thank You for swimming fishies
and sweet birds that sing.
Thank You, God, for bouncing bunnies
and every living thing.

Jesus Shine Through Me

Jesus, work and shine through me,
just like the brightest light.
Guide each step I take today
and help me do what's right.
So, when I show my acts of love,
everyone will see,
that Jesus lives within my heart
and works through little me.

"Let your light so shine before men, that they may see your good works, and glorify your Father which is in Heaven."
Matthew 5:16

Prayer for Healing

I pray for those who are sick or poor.
Jesus, watch over them a little bit more.
Make their bodies healthy and strong,
please don't let this sickness last very long.
One touch from Your hand, so loving and pure,
can bring about an instant cure.
I stand in faith, and I believe
in the healing that they will receive.

"My dear friend, I pray that You are doing fine in every way and that your health is good."
3 John 1:2

"Wisdom begins with respect for the Lord."
Psalm 111:10

Prayer for School

Jesus, bless our school today,
my teachers and my friends.
Please fill us with Your wisdom,
to listen well and understand.
Be in all we do and say,
in the classroom and when we play.
Send Your mighty angels
to keep us safe throughout the day.

"For I know the plans I have for you, declares the Lord,
plans to prosper you and not to harm you,
plans to give you hope and a future."
Jeremiah 29:11

How God Sees Me

The mirror says I am weak,
but You say I'm strong
The nurse says I'm too sick,
but You say, "Just hold on!"
In sports, Coach says I'm not enough,
but You say, "Nah, your heart is tough!"
Good grades at school are often rare,
but You say keep studying, I'll get there.
I'm starting to receive, to bashfully believe
all the good You say of me.
Jesus, help me find my worth in You
until your version of me comes true!

"Go everywhere in the world.
Tell the Good News to everyone."
Mark 16:15

Tell People About Jesus

I want to tell the whole wide world
how wonderful You are.
Show me how to spread Your word
on Earth both near and far.
People need to hear the truth
the Bible tells of Jesus' love.
You died and rose so we could live
with You in Heaven up above.

God Listens to Me

Jesus, You're listening
to every word I say.
I don't have to close my eyes
or kneel down when I pray.
Even when I think a prayer,
You hear it and respond with care.
You listen to the simple things
that pop up in my mind
and dreams tucked deep within my heart,
that no one else can find.
I know You're always with me,
You've given me Your word.
Thank You Lord, that every prayer I pray
never goes unheard.

Prayer for My Friends

Jesus, bless my friends today.
Thank You for the fun and games we play.
Lead them toward the way that's right.
Keep them safe both day and night.
Help them to remember
they can always count on You.
To guide them and protect them
in everything they do.

Prayer When I'm Worried

God, You hold the world in Your hands,
including little me.
But today I feel overcome
with doubt and anxiety.
You know what's in my mind and heart,
so You know what I am worried about.
You tell me it will be okay,
because You already know the way.
Can You please help my mind to rest
and focus on all the ways I'm blessed.

"Don't worry about anything; instead, pray about everything. Tell God what You need and thank him for all he has done."
Philippians 4:6

"Let them give thanks to the Lord."
Psalm 107:8

Thanksgiving Prayer

As friends and family gather 'round,
we have so much to share.
We thank You, God, for times like this,
to show how much we care.
Thank You for this meal,
and the hands that prepared it with love.
For every gift Your goodness sends
from Heaven up above.

Mealtime Prayer

Thank You for the food we eat,
that makes us strong and able.
We remember all the blessings You give,
as we sit around this table.
As we close our eyes and bow our head,
we thank You for our daily bread.
Jesus, come and be our guest
and let this food to us be blessed.

Prayer for Creation

Today I stopped and looked around
because I thought I heard a sound.
The Bible says even the rocks cry out
whenever God is walking about.
Shh! Listen! There it went again,
a noise where Angels may just have been.
Pronouncing, announcing, "Make way for the King!"
God's on the move, causing Creation to Sing!
May we join in, with hearts full of praise,
our loving Creator shines in every place.

"All the Earth worships you. They sing praises to Your name."
Psalm 66:4

"I praise You because You made me in an amazing and wonderful way. What You have done is wonderful. I know this very well."
Psalm 139:14

Jesus' Masterpiece

When I feel self-conscious about how I look or speak,
I remember You purposely made me unique.
You designed me with gifts made only for me.
You knit me together so wonderfully.
If I am different, help me be proud of myself,
and not try to be like everyone else.
I want to become who You created me to be,
Jesus' friend and masterpiece.

When I'm Feeling Sad

When my day goes wrong and I'm feeling down,
and it seems like things won't turn around,
I remember that You are always near
and will wipe away my every tear.
You always listen and understand,
then guide me with Your loving hand.
You make my darkest days shine bright
and turn my sadness to delight.

"Don't let your hearts be troubled. Trust in God. And trust in Me."
John 14:1

Christmas Prayer

I have a special Christmas prayer
of thanks to God above,
for sending Jesus, the greatest gift,
the reflection of Your love.
The star shined bright, the angels sang,
and kings bowed down at the power of His name.
So, we celebrate Jesus this night of His birth,
the most amazing treasure God ever sent to Earth.

Jesus, My Savior

Thank You, Jesus, for Your saving grace.
For erasing my sin and taking my place.
How can I show my gratitude?
By giving my life for You to make new.
Teach me how to love others the way that You do,
so I can be a mirror of You.
Jesus, my Savior, I'm running my race,
until the day comes when I see Your sweet face.

"For the wages of sin is death,
but the gift of God is eternal life in Christ Jesus."
Romans 6:23

Singing God's Praises

I sing to You with notes of praise,
to lift Your heart and magnify Your name.
Let my whole life be a song
of thanksgiving to God all day long.
Oh, what a sweet melody,
when I sing of the grace You've shown to me.
Let my music bring You glory and love
and fill the Heavens up above.

Awaken Little Warrior

God, You chose someone very small
to fight a giant nine feet tall.
You helped small David fight and win.
You gave him strength and fought for him.
You can do the same for me.
Awaken this little warrior You see.
With You at my side, I will be brave,
and step forward into the plans You've made.

Prayer When I Feel Lonely

Lord, I feel so lonely all of the time
even surrounded by people, I'm lonely inside.
Something feels broken, my smile is upside down.
Then You came along and gave me a crown.
You took away the empty by becoming my friend,
One who stays by me right to the end.
I feel better already, just knowing You're for me
I can't wait to tell others our amazing love story.

"I will never leave you; I will never abandon you."
Hebrews 13:5

Jesus Loves Me

You made the stars and oceans deep
and said that none compares to me.
I am Your treasure and greatest prize,
You know my name, You made my eyes.
You love me on good days and bad ones too,
nothing can separate me from You.
How cool is it to have as my biggest fan,
the King of Heaven, the Great I AM!

"If you declare with your mouth, 'Jesus is Lord,' and if you believe in your heart, then you will be saved."
Romans 10:9

My Prayer to Receive Jesus

Jesus, I believe You are God's son
and died for all my sins.
I'm sorry for the things I've done,
please come into my heart to live.
Be the leader of my life
and wash me white as snow.
You are my Lord and Savior;
I'll follow wherever you go.

Cover your little ones in God's love with this soft, cuddly prayer blanket to go with the prayer book.
Available now at www.churchdog.org

WWW.CHURCHDOG.ORG

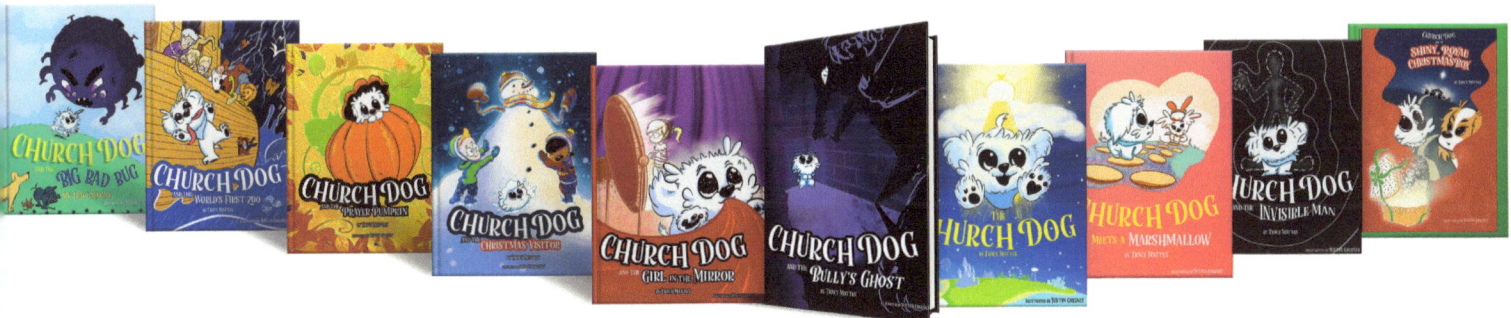

For more exciting details about the Award Winning Church Dog Adventure Series go to www.churchdog.org

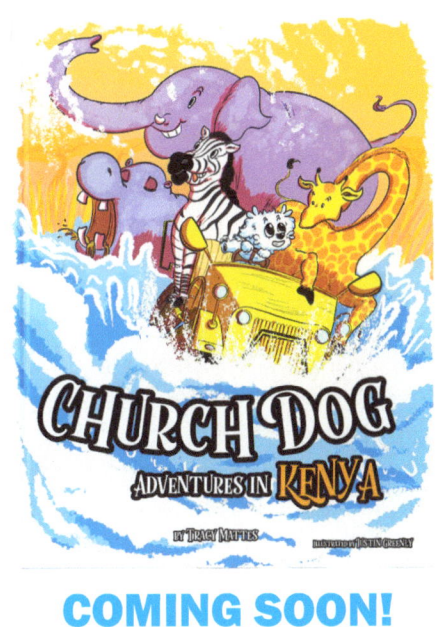

COMING SOON!

Award Winning

About the Author

Tracy Mattes has been part of the Olympic Family for more than 25 years. Her passion has always been to share the values of sport with young children. Mattes was Director of Global Programs for the World Olympians Association and served in nine Olympic Games in various capacities within the organization. She also worked for sport National Governing Body Foundations, including seven years as Executive Director for the USA Water Ski & Wake Sports Foundation. As a competitive athlete, Mattes, a five-time All American, specialized in the 400-meter hurdles, ranking 7th in the world and was inducted into three Halls of Fame.

Mattes' career has taken her to more than 74 countries around the world. In 2005, she was selected as a United Nations Special Representative specializing in the advancement of young children through the values of education and sport. This unique global perspective comes through in her writing. She also has worked as a news producer and editor at three NBC affiliates. In 2010, Mattes won one of the top prizes at the 28th Milan International FICTS Film Festival for her documentary film "The Power of Education through Sport" which she produced, edited and narrated. For her efforts as a world class athlete and her humanitarian work, Mattes was honored by being inducted into the World Sport Humanitarian Hall of Fame in 2009.

She received her bachelor's degree in Broadcast Journalism from Arizona State University and her master's degree in International Business from the International University of Monaco in 2006 and was Valedictorian of her graduating class. Tracy has always shared her strong Christian faith throughout her career and she currently serves in a leadership position at Community Presbyterian Church in Celebration, Florida, the picturesque town that Disney built. Mattes lives there with her two Maltese dogs, K'noot and Marshmallow, who can hear the Church bells from their balcony.

www.ingramcontent.com/pod-product-compliance
Lightning Source LLC
Chambersburg PA
CBHW040722060526
44119CB00083B/300